TURNER'S ITALY

Christopher Baker

TURNER'S ITALY

National Galleries of Scotland
Edinburgh · 2009

Introduction

J. M.W. Turner (1775–1851) was fascinated by the experience of different countries and cultures across Europe, finding inspiration for his work from as far afield as the Western Isles of Scotland and Vienna. But it was Italy and its art and architecture that always held a special place in his affections. The richness and diversity of Italy's climate, landscapes, cities and customs were reflected in many of his finest paintings, which range from unforgettable images of the splendour of Rome, to smouldering sunsets over the rooftops of Venice.

There was a long tradition of British artists and collectors travelling to Italy as part of a Grand Tour of Europe, but such journeys were usually undertaken only once, as an adventure to complete an education. Travelling to Italy in the early nineteenth century could take many days and involve discomfort and danger; in fact Turner was twice involved in coach crashes when crossing the Alps, and armed himself with a sword hidden in his umbrella because of the threat of bandits. Nonetheless, he made seven European tours which included visits to Italy, in 1802, 1819, 1828–9, 1833, 1836, 1840 and 1843. This sustained enthusiasm, in spite of the obstacles that had to be overcome, illustrates the depth of his interest in the country and the extent of the inspiration it provided. Because his journeys span much of his career, focusing on Turner's Italian work allows an overview of his evolution as an artist, and the transition he made from early, conventional landscape studies, to the emotive and visionary pictures of his later years.

The onslaught of mass tourism had not yet begun, and so Turner could not only delight in all he saw, but also exploit it on his return to Britain. He used studies of Rome, Venice, and many smaller cities, to inspire the two most successful aspects of his career: the creation of ambitious oil paintings which were exhibited annually, and the production of watercolours that were engraved for publication, so spreading his vision far beyond his gallery-going audience. Turner never matched the clichéd 'romantic' image of an artist – a lone figure only driven by his vocation and unconcerned by the market for his work. He knew his worth and had a sound sense of self-promotion and business skill, prompted perhaps by a desire to rise above his humble origins as the son of a Covent Garden barber, which he succeeded in doing with remarkable speed.

JOS?. WILL?. MALLORD TURNER.

[1] George Dance,
*Joseph Mallord William
Turner*, 1800
Royal Academy of Arts,
London

Italy Imagined

Turner's fascination with Italian culture developed initially when, as a young man in London, he studied oil paintings, watercolours, sculptures, prints and books which gave a taste of the sites and treasures of Italy. He visited important private art collections and attended exhibitions and auctions, discovering the work of artists such as Titian, Veronese, Claude, Poussin and Piranesi. It was above all Claude's idealised vision of Italy that was to influence Turner's work [2]. Turner's respect for Claude was based on the fact that he shared the earlier artist's ambition to explore fully the poetic possibilities of landscape as a serious subject for art. He took from Claude an interest in classical subjects, an awareness of how to structure his works, and an appreciation of how to depict the dazzling sunlight of Mediterranean ports and landscapes. Turner then gradually taught himself how to enrich these elements with remarkably bold handling of paint and exploration of brilliant colour.

[2] Claude Lorrain, *Landscape with Apollo and the Musēs*, 1652
National Gallery of Scotland, Edinburgh

< [3] *Rome: The Tiber with the Aventine on the Left*, 1794–7 (detail)
National Gallery of Scotland, Edinburgh

British artists such as John Robert Cozens and Richard Wilson who had already made the pilgrimage to Italy, and themselves drawn inspiration from Claude, also fired Turner's enthusiasm to travel to the warm south. But, at this early stage in his career he could only journey to Italy in his imagination by closely studying their work. A watercolour, such as *Rome: The Tiber with the Aventine on the Left* [3], shows Turner replicating the delicate colour washes in blue and grey which Cozens had employed during his own visits to Italy some twenty years earlier.

The study of Italy and its art was also promoted by the Royal Academy of Arts, the teaching and exhibiting institution Turner was most closely allied to. The Academy placed an overwhelming emphasis on the experience of classical and Renaissance Italy as the source of artistic wisdom. Turner was admitted to the Royal Academy Schools in 1789, and made drawings after its collection of plaster casts of classical sculpture. In 1799 he was elected an Associate Academician, a distinction celebrated in a delicate portrait study by George Dance [1], which depicts him as a dapper figure, on the cusp of celebrity. Two years later Turner became a full Royal Academician, the youngest ever elected. He was still only twenty-seven.

Italy: 1802

From the earliest years of his career, travel was essential to Turner's working procedures and success. He journeyed across Britain, in an unrelenting search for new experiences and vistas, which he recorded in pencil in his many sketchbooks. His tours of Wales and Scotland had whetted his appetite for dramatic, mountainous scenery, but it was not until 1802 when a brief period of peace brought stability to war-torn Europe that he was able to cross the Channel, and make his way through France and over the Alps into Italy. In an atmospheric drawing in chalk and watercolour [4] he recorded his impression of Aosta, just over the border. Its buildings, such as the triumphal arch on the left, which is dedicated to the Emperor Augustus, from whom the city takes its name, gave Turner a first tantalising taste of the grandeur of ancient Rome.

The journey that Turner made in 1802 had been funded by three important patrons: Lord Yarborough, the Earl of Darlington and Walter Fawkes. Turner tended to attract very loyal supporters from both the landed aristocracy and urban moneyed classes. Although they had varying tastes, one of the things that connected them was their knowledge of the classical inheritance (in the form of sculpture, architecture, history and poetry), and the art of the Renaissance. Furthermore, some of them had undertaken their own Italian tours, and so Turner's ambitions to explore and exploit Italian culture matched their expectations about what a great artist should achieve.

The resumption of war and his professional commitments meant that Turner was not able to return to Italy until 1819. However, he continued to depict the country, using as his inspiration the work of other artists. Turner painted with such ingenuity and conviction that anyone viewing his works of this period could easily be forgiven for assuming he had spent many years on the spot scrutinising his subjects. He created impressive illustrations for travel books, including *A Picturesque Tour of Italy*, published by John Murray in 1820, and a study of Pompeii. The illustrations intended for the latter were eventually engraved for a

[4] *Aosta: The Arch of Augustus, Looking South to Mt Emilius*, 1802
Tate, London

< [5] *Bay of Naples (Vesuvius Angry)*, *c.*1817 (detail)
Williamson Art Gallery, Birkenhead

9

book entitled *Friendships Offering* published in 1830, and included a pair of contrasting watercolours: *Bay of Naples (Vesuvius in Repose)* (Private Collection) and *Bay of Naples (Vesuvius Angry)* [5]. The more dramatic of the two works, *Bay of Naples (Vesuvius Angry)*, shows a stunning volcanic eruption, a pyrotechnic display which floods the image with orange and golden light. Turner was never to see such an event, but the prospect of natural wonders of this sort must have spurred him on to tour Italy. Further encouragement came in 1817 with the publication of the fourth section of Lord Byron's epic poem *Childe Harold's Pilgrimage*, which features rhapsodic descriptions of Venice. Always sensitive to poetry, Turner would have been inspired by the prospect of seeing cities in which '… structures rise, / As from the stroke of the enchanters wand …'

Rome: 1819, 1828

On 1 August 1819 Turner left London. His goal was Rome and he journeyed via Turin, Milan, Venice and Bologna, making numerous pencil studies in his sketchbooks; in total he filled twenty-three of them during this tour, building a great store of experience, which could be recalled for future use. Cities and landscapes, monuments and street scenes, were all worthy of his close attention. He also took a serious interest in ancient Roman remains and carefully transcribed the inscriptions on those that he encountered along his route. The knowledge Turner had acquired which formed the backdrop to this scholarly approach is revealed by what remains of his library. It includes works of history and art history, as well classical literary sources and guidebooks. He was an attentive reader, sketching ideas at the edge of pages, and sometimes writing commentaries on issues he found of interest or with which he disagreed.

Turner arrived in Rome on 4 or 5 October, and the city did not disappoint. The profusion of ancient remains and Renaissance and Baroque churches and palaces, and the sheer drama of its setting, fired his imagination. He made numerous drawings in the Vatican, the Forum, and all over the seven hills of the city. He also worked on a splendid sequence of watercolours, which may have been intended as the basis for a published series of works, although this ambition was never realised. Studies such as his *Ruins in Rome: View from the Palatine* [6] must have been worked on in the open air; in this case Turner created a very unconventional view of the hill dominated by the ruins of the palaces of the emperors. He was evidently

[6] *Ruins in Rome:*
View from the Palatine, 1819
Tate, London

[7] *The Castel dell'Ovo,*
Naples with Capri and Sorrento in
the Distance: Early Morning, 1819
Tate, London

fascinated by a decorative jumble of abandoned ancient sculptural fragments, below wind-swept trees and a stormy sky.

Turner absorbed much of what Rome had to offer and also became part of the large number of English men and women who were in the city in the autumn of 1819. Two weeks after his arrival and keen to continue exploring, he travelled on to Tivoli, and then south to Naples, Sorrento, Amalfi and Paestum, drawing and working in watercolour, all the way. Among his finest works of this period are studies such as his view of the Castel dell'Ovo in the heart of the Bay of Naples [7]. This remarkably austere and ethereal image shows sunlight glancing off the fifteenth-century building, perhaps at the beginning of the day.

On his return to London in January 1820, Turner was brimming with ideas about how to express the profundity of the experiences he had enjoyed. Just over two months after his return from Italy he showed *Rome from the Vatican* [8] at the Royal Academy exhibition. This great panorama encapsulates the inspiration that the direct experience of the artistic wealth and light of Rome had provided. Turner's

[8] *Rome from the Vatican. Raffaelle, Accompanied by La Fornarina, Preparing his Pictures for the Decoration of the Loggia*, 1820
Tate, London

picture was painted on the three-hundredth anniversary of the death of the great Renaissance artist Raphael, who is shown in the foreground, glancing thoughtfully at his frescoes in the vaults above, which form part of a complex perspectival scheme that draws attention back and forth across the composition. By connecting his work with Raphael's, Turner was not only displaying his admiration for the most exalted of old master painters, but also conveying his own soaring ambitions. Raphael is depicted in the company of his mistress, La Fornarina, who is engaged in the frivolous business of admiring her jewels in the sunshine. These playful references to Renaissance art are overlaid with seventeenth-century achievements: the landscape painting at the lower left is reminiscent of the works of Claude, and beyond can be seen the great Piazza before St Peter's, with its embracing colonnade designed by Bernini. A religious procession enters the Piazza. The cityscape on the far side of it is dominated by the Castel S. Angelo, and the view extends to the snow-capped mountains on the horizon, beneath an arc of searing blue sky. *Rome from the Vatican* can be seen as a manifesto, expressing Turner's passion for Italy and its complex, layered, artistic heritage.

Adopting a high viewpoint as he did with his Vatican fantasy was a device Turner employed for many of his city views. It was ideal for conveying a sense of scale and civic grandeur and encouraging comparison with maps and plans, so that buildings might be identified. He used such an approach for a view of Florence, which was also based on sketches made in 1819, although worked up later in watercolour [9]. This composition proved so popular that Turner created four versions of it. He allows us to look towards the setting sun along the River Arno, taking in the Ponte Vecchio, and the Palazzo della Signoria and Duomo at the right. The figures idling in the foreground, their musical instruments discarded, convey a mood of reverie and indulgence.

Turner returned to Rome in 1828, living there for three months, but on this occasion with quite a different agenda in mind. He was now aged fifty-three and did not dash around the city recording everything that delighted his eye, but rather engaged further in the social life that Rome had to offer, and found himself a studio in which to paint. The significance of this cannot be underestimated, as there was no other point during Turner's long career of travelling all over the Continent when he chose to settle down and paint ambitious works in oil; this was a practice always confined to his London studio.

He worked in a building just off the Corso, and the pictures he produced

[9] *Florence from San Miniato*, *c.*1827
The Herbert Art Gallery and Museum, Coventry

[10] *Palestrina – Composition*, 1828
Tate, London

during his stay differed widely in terms of scale and subject matter, suggesting that Turner was trying to demonstrate to his Roman audience the breadth of his accomplishments. They included a beautiful, although conventional depiction of the town of Orvieto, and an ambitious figurative painting exploring the myth of Medea. The picture Turner worked on first was his *Palestrina – Composition* [10], painted for his patron Lord Egremont, although never in fact delivered to him, and probably not finished until Turner's return to London. It may be intended both as a view of Palestrina, the hill town east of Rome, and a homage to the composer Pierluigi da Palestrina (1525–1594), whose birthplace it was, and a biography of whom was published around the time Turner was painting the work. The glowing town clings to the slopes at the left and almost takes on the appearance of a spectral or heavenly city. The picture was first exhibited in Edinburgh at the Royal Scottish Academy in 1845. A critic writing in *The Scotsman* declared '…there is something very grand and splendid in the effect of the whole, as viewed from a little distance … Turner is a singular man, and he has shown his possession of that highest of all gifts, originality…'

Although he often received praise in Britain which emphasised how his work stood apart from that of all his contemporaries, in Rome its startling novelty led to disdain. Towards the end of his stay in the city Turner organised an exhibition of his paintings at the Palazzo Trulli on the Quirinal Hill. It was greeted with bewilderment, and prompted criticism of him producing works 'in the English Mylord-taste of Anglican fantasy' and of his 'flogged painting' technique. It is, however, unlikely that Turner was particularly troubled by this as he was enjoying the company of a coterie of British artists and travellers, as well as members of the Accademia di San Luca (the Artists' Academy). He had joined the Accademia as an honorary member in 1819, thanks to a recommendation from the pre-eminent

[11] *A Villa (Villa Madama – Moonlight),* *c.* 1826–7
Tate, London

neoclassical sculptor Antonio Canova (1757–1822). The two artists might be considered worlds apart in terms of their work, but they probably met in London in 1815, and clearly had a sincere mutual respect; Canova considered Turner a 'great genius'.

It was clearly important to sustain such illustrious connections, but to develop his wider reputation Turner also had to continue with his printmaking projects, arranging the production of engravings after his watercolours, and contributing illustrations to books. One of the most attractive publications he worked on in the 1820s was the travel poem entitled *Italy* by Samuel Rogers (1763–1855). Rogers, whose wealth derived from banking, was a collector, patron, host and wit. He first published his poem in 1822, and then commissioned a new luxurious edition which was eventually produced in 1830, and proved a great success. It featured twenty-five vignettes that were designed by Turner and other artists. Turner's contributions included memorable works such as his nocturnal study, *A Villa (Villa Madama – Moonlight)* [11], a romanticised view of the building designed by Raphael and his followers on the outskirts of Rome. His great achievement in such images was to compress into a tiny space a compelling sense of atmosphere and incident.

It was during the 1820s that Turner's Italian experiences began to have a profound influence on his British works. He was engaged with a number of lucrative projects which involved depicting English, Welsh, and Scottish landscapes. Many of them were seen by Turner through the prism of Italy; he constructed them using Claudian compositions, and bathed them in Mediterranean light. A work such as his study of Minehead [12] effectively illustrates this approach. It shows the seaside resort in Somerset but could easily be mistaken for a view of part of the Bay of Naples.

[12] *Minehead, Somersetshire, c.*1820
Lady Lever Art Gallery, National Museums Liverpool

Maturity: 1836

During the 1830s Turner made two further visits to Italy – in 1833 to Venice, and in 1836 to Turin. The latter journey was undertaken with the Scottish landowner and collector Hugh Andrew Johnstone Munro of Novar (1797–1864), the only patron of Turner's actually to travel with him to Italy. Novar and Turner had been friends since the mid-1820s. Over the following decades Novar was to build one of the greatest collections of Turner's oil paintings and watercolours ever assembled, which included many works that explore Italian themes. However, the warm friendship that they enjoyed went far beyond the business of buying and selling

[13] *The Fountain of Indolence*, 1834
The Beaverbrook Art Gallery, The Beaverbrook
Foundation, New Brunswick

pictures and was sustained until the end of Turner's life. Novar was an amateur artist and their 1836 journey became a sketching trip with Turner taking on the role of a mentor. As they travelled down through the Val D'Aosta into Italy his teaching revealed some of the secrets of his own artistic practice:

> [Turner's] *sketches were rapid, and with the aid of his tremendous memory were completed subsequently, at leisure, in the inn... his touch was so sure and decisive, and his materials were of the rudest – brushes worn away to a single hair, and now thrice as valuable as when they were new.*

Turner was never again to travel to Rome, but because of his 'tremendous memory' and the great store of knowledge he had built up in his sketchbooks, it continued to inspire a number of the finest works during the last twenty years of his career. In 1834 he had returned to the themes of Roman myth and history with paintings such *The Fountain of Indolence* [13]. Its subject may have been suggested by the Scottish poet James Thomson's *The Castle of Indolence* (1748), which describes a stronghold of enchantment, including a high spouting fountain, which has to yield to a 'Knight of Industry'. Turner valued Thomson's work, but has created here a rich, imaginative vision of a leisured, and perhaps decadent ancient Roman society, all of his own.

Later in the 1830s Turner changed direction and focused on the contrast between 'modern' Italy and the ancient world, and explored the theme of the rise and fall of great civilisations. In 1838 he painted *Ancient Italy – Ovid banished from Rome* (Private Collection), and as a foil for it produced *Modern Italy – the Pifferari* [14]. This work focuses on Tivoli, about thirty kilometers from Rome, at the edge of the Sabine hills, and shows a breathtaking view across the Roman Campagna. Here is a Christian rather than pagan world, and so at the right a religious procession makes its way towards a shrine, while at the left a monk hears confession at the roadside. Just beyond him are the *pifferari*, travelling musicians, who played bagpipes and *pifferi* (a type of oboe), and converged on Rome each Christmas to pay homage to the Virgin. The Scottish artist, Sir David Wilkie had depicted them in a painting of 1829 (Royal Collection), and it is possible that Turner knew of his work, and borrowed his theme from it.

Monro of Novar bought *Modern Italy – the Pifferari* from the artist, and also acquired an outstanding painting Turner produced in the following year: *Modern Rome – Campo Vaccino* [15]. This picture perhaps looks as though it is

[14] *Modern Italy – the Pifferari*, 1838

Kelvingrove Art Gallery and Museum, Glasgow

[15] *Modern Rome – Campo Vaccino*, 1839
The Rosebery Collection, on loan to the National Gallery
of Scotland, Edinburgh

[16] *Dogana, and Madonna della Salute, Venice*, 1843
National Gallery of Art, Washington D C, given in memory of
Governor Alvan T. Fuller by The Fuller Foundation Inc.

a celebration of the ancient, rather than modern city. However, it was painted by Turner as a counterpoint to a work now in the Tate, which features a reconstruction of ancient Rome, used as a backdrop for the story of Agrippina and the Ashes of Germanicus. In *Modern Rome* the fabric of the past has crumbled, and we are shown an anthology of spectacular ruins, interspersed with Baroque churches; goats are milked in the foreground, and a tiny figure, perhaps an archaeologist, ascends a ladder to study a column at the right. The city beyond is depicted in an astounding palette of pastel hues – delicate pinks, yellows, mauves and oranges – as though dreamed rather than seen, at the end of the day. The whole image is a deeply poetic recollection, and was connected by Turner with a verse from Lord Byron's *Childe Harold's Pilgrimage*:

> *The moon is up and yet it is not night,*
> *The sun as yet divides the day with her*

Although Turner never met Byron he developed a profound empathy with his achievement, and appended lines from his poems to six of his paintings when they were exhibited.

Venice: 1819, 1833, 1840

Turner made a far greater commitment to the study of Rome than Venice, and yet it is his Venetian works which are perhaps more widely known and admired. He has come to be seen as one of the great interpreters of Venice, through his ability to convey and celebrate the city's allure and melancholy. The shifting, insubstantial qualities of Venice – the result of light dancing on water and architecture – were perhaps the perfect subjects for him to address with his box of watercolours. Turner also proved however, to be able to translate these phenomena into brilliant essays achieved with oil paint. There are no shortage of precedents with which his Venetian work might be compared, ranging from the eighteenth-century views of Canaletto, to those of contemporaries such as Clarkson Stanfield and William Etty. All their paintings however deal with crisp certainties: perspective, texture, outline and detail. Turner almost always took quite a different approach, searching for an elusive Venice, often slightly abstracted and invariably gloriously coloured [16].

He made his first visit in 1819, staying for about eight days, when on his way to Rome, and worked on a number of pencil studies as well as four watercolours.

[17] *The Doge's Palace from the Bacino*, 1840
Walker Art Gallery, National Museums Liverpool

Turner journeyed to the city again in the late summer of 1833, remaining this time for ten days and dashing off on average about twenty pencil sketches a day. The final and most productive Venetian visit was made in 1840, by which time he was sixty-five. He arrived in the city on 20 August and stayed until 3 September. Turner explored the city by foot and in gondolas, studying it by day and night, enjoying terrific electric storms and sultry calms. He depicted the famous sites – views of the Doge's Palace and San Marco, and the Grand Canal thronged with craft [17] – but arguably some of his greatest works from this period of intense creativity are more unconventional, informal images.

He stayed on the third floor of the Hotel Europa in the Palazzo Giustiniani, near the entrance to the Grand Canal, and made his room the subject of one the most original of all his Venetian studies [18]. It shows a rather grand apartment with a painted ceiling and fabric hung on the walls, and a clear view of the Campanile of S. Marco at the left. The yellow curtain at the right perhaps enclosed his bed. Everything is reduced to suggestive, tremulous fields of colour. The roof of the hotel proved to be a fine vantage point from which to establish other unusual views of the city. These include a carefully orchestrated depiction of the campanili

of the churches of San Marco, San Moise and Santo Stefano [19], in which dawn provides the backdrop for the city's terracotta roofs. At canal level, very rapidly worked nocturnal studies provide a fascinating contrast to such sunlit scenes. In *The Salute from the Traghetto del Ridotto* [20] Turner used the dark tonality of red-brown paper as a foil for the lantern which marks the landing stage where gondolas are moored. A crescent moon can just be seen above the dark profile of the great Baroque church.

The many drawings and watercolours created during Turner's explorations of the city were used to inspire some of his finest late oil paintings. In *Approach*

[19] *Venice: Looking North from the Hotel Europa, with the Campaniles of San Marco, San Moise and Santo Stefano*, 1840
Tate, London

to Venice [21] the city appears as a mirage, hovering between sea and sky. It sent Turner's great champion, the critic John Ruskin, into ecstasies: '...it was, I think, when I first saw it, the most perfectly beautiful piece of colour of all that I have seen produced by human hands, by any means, or at any period.' It was Ruskin who, along with Turner, did so much to place Venice at the forefront of the British perception of Italy and its attractions. His three volume work *The Stones of Venice* which aroused considerable interest with the Victorian public, was a celebration of the art and architecture of the city, in which he considered its buildings as models of Byzantine, Gothic and Renaissance style. The first volume was published in the last year of Turner's life, and the copy Ruskin presented to him survives as part of the artist's library; Ruskin inscribed it: *J. M. W. Turner Esq: R.A. / with the Authors affectionate / & respectful regards.* Sadly, Turner's reaction to it is not recorded.

[20] *Venice: The Salute from the Traghetto del Ridotto, c.*1840
Tate, London

[21] *Approach to Venice*, 1844
National Gallery of Art, Washington DC,
Andrew W. Mellon Collection

Late Works

In 1843 Turner undertook a late summer tour of Switzerland, which involved travelling over the border to visit the north Italian lakes. His journey was curtailed due to illness. Turner's health deteriorated further in 1845, but he continued working with astounding vigour and invention right up until his death in 1851. It was with his pictures of these years that he pushed back conventional boundaries, sometimes working in a remarkably physical manner, using palette knives, rags and his hands, as well as a brush, to manipulate thickly textured (impastoed) paint, and on other occasions exploring astoundingly bold combinations of colour, which over one hundred and fifty years later have lost none of their power to startle and intrigue.

Turner used a very fiery palette for his depiction of the myth of *Glaucus and Scylla* [22] of 1841, entirely appropriately as it is a tale of consuming passions. In the background Mount Etna on Sicily can just be seen smoking. The complex narrative enacted before it is drawn from Ovid's *Metamorphoses*. Glaucus, a sea god, loved Scylla, but she scorned him, and in the painting flees from him. He had appealed to the sorceress Circe for help, but on hearing his plea Circe fell in love with Glaucus herself and decided to punish Scylla. Her lower body was changed into frightful monsters and she plunged into the sea between Italy and Sicily, and was transformed into treacherous rocks. Turner contrasts this grand operatic tragedy with a touch of verisimilitude on the shoreline, delicately depicting there a crab and shells.

It seems likely that he conceived *Glaucus and Scylla* as a pendant or companion picture to the *Dawn of Christianity (Flight into Egypt)* [23]. Both works were exhibited at the Royal Academy in 1841 and bought by the important Turner collector G.B. Windus. The two paintings create a striking contrast between pagan and Christian worlds, the bedrock of Italian civilisation, depicted in hot and cool colours. Here the Holy Family can be seen fleeing on the riverbank at the right. Their flight is incongruously set before snowy mountains, and the serpent refers to mankind's fall in Eden, from which Christ will offer redemption.

The most daring of all Turner's paintings were not those created to be exhibited, or made with a patron in mind, but rather the ones he produced in his final years for himself. After a lifetime of working so successfully for the

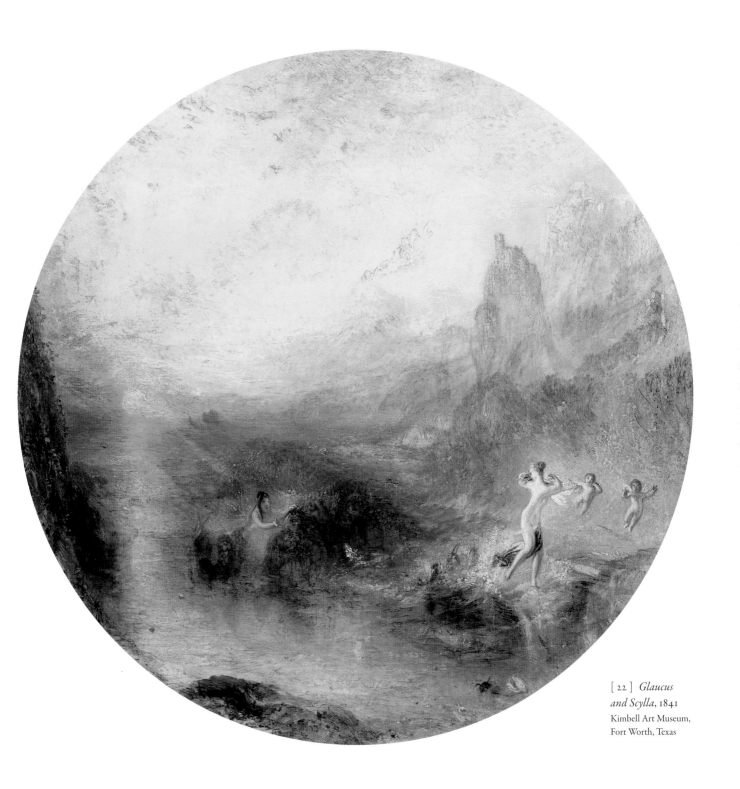

[22] *Glaucus and Scylla*, 1841
Kimbell Art Museum,
Fort Worth, Texas

[23] *Dawn of Christianity (Flight into Egypt)*, 1841
Ulster Museum, Belfast

market, he became a truly experimental artist exploring private themes, re-visiting favourite subjects, and blurring expectations about what might be considered 'finished' or 'unfinished'. His painting *The Val d'Aosta* [24], which must date from the late 1840s, exemplifies this approach. It is a heavily textured and energetically worked canvas, in which the mountains and sky appear to fuse in a maelstrom of light. Its traditional title, if reliable, connects it with key moments in his relationship with Italy – his 1802 visit to Aosta, when he first visited the country, and his 1836 journey through the Val d'Aosta with his good friend Munro of Novar. These seminal experiences may be recalled here in a wholly original, visionary work.

Whether working on enigmatic paintings such as this, or more easily legible pictures, Turner perhaps used Italy to feed his desire for imaginative escapes from many of the harsh realities of nineteenth-century Britain. Exploring myth, history and personal recollection he created intoxicating works which are now more highly valued than ever before.

[24] *The Val d'Aosta, c.*1840–50
National Gallery of Victoria, Melbourne, Australia, purchased with the assistance of a special grant from the Government of Victoria

35

Turner & Italy

If you have enjoyed this souvenir guide
and would like more information, the
book which accompanies the exhibition
is available from: NGS Publishing,
Scottish National Gallery of Modern Art,
Belford Road, Edinburgh EH4 3DR or
www.nationalgalleries.com

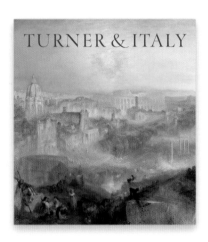

Published by the Trustees of the National Galleries
of Scotland to accompany the exhibition *Turner & Italy*
held at the National Gallery Complex, Edinburgh,
from 27 March to 7 June 2009, organised by the National
Gallery of Scotland and Ferrara Arte in collaboration
with the Museum of Fine Arts, Budapest.

© The Trustees of the National Galleries of Scotland 2009

All illustrations are reproduced courtesy of the
lending institutions.

ISBN 978 1 906270 21 6

Designed & typeset by Dalrymple in Garamond Premier
Printed on Chromomatt 150gsm by Woods of Perth

Front cover: detail from *Dogana, and Madonna della
Salute, Venice*, 1843 [16]

Back cover: *Rome, from Mount Aventine*, 1836
The Earl of Rosebery, on loan to the National Gallery
of Scotland, Edinburgh

Page 1: *The Rialto Bridge from the Albergo Leone Bianco*
from the 'Milan to Venice' sketchbook, 1819, Tate, London

Frontispiece: *Venice: Santa Maria della Salute with the
Traghetto San Maurizio*, 1840, Tate, London

*The proceeds from the sale of this book go towards
supporting the National Galleries of Scotland, a charity
registered in Scotland (no.SC003278).*